MW01098194

# Come, Grandma!
by Kristine Goodan

To Waylon, K., from his Grandma, Birdie!

© 2022 Kristine Goodan

Come, Grandma!

by Kristine Goodan
Illustrations by Thäis Armstrong

"Come, Grandma! I found a nest!
A huge nest in that tree,
 way up high."

"That's a Bald Eagle's nest, Waylon.
Do you see the eagle sitting in the nest?
That's the Mom sitting on her eggs.
Pretty soon the eggs will hatch,
and we'll see how many eaglets she has.
See her white head?
Her babies won't look like that.

Let's look at the calendar.
January, February, March, April, May.
 That's where we are now, in May."

"Come, Grandma. I think that it's
time to look at the nest again."

"Waylon, I think that you're right!
Do you hear that squawking sound?
I think that we have an eaglet,
but I can't see anything. What is the date?"

"Come, Grandma.
I see TWO heads peeking out.
Wow, what a racket they are making.
They must be hungry."

" Grandma, why is the Mommy eagle sleeping in that tree? Why isn't she in the nest?"

"Oh , Waylon. She is tired, very tired.
She is trying to sleep while she can before
she has to feed those two babies."

"Doesn't the Dad help? Where is he?"

"Let's try to find him.  Oh, yes, he is flying over there. He is looking for fish to feed those hungry eaglets.
Watch now. He is landing in that Fir tree with a Flounder. We call that the feeding branch. He is now eating part of the fish."

"Cool, Grandma." "Now I see him.
And now he is flying to the nest with the rest of the fish to share. "

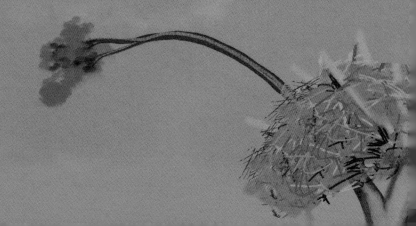

"Look, Grandma. Can we give names to the eaglets?
I see one of them climbing up the side branch of the tree.
He can be Firsty. Now he's flapping his wings. Is he going to fly?"

"Not today. He's exercising his wings so that he can fly a little later.
Do you see how BIG he is and how dark?
He is larger than his Mom, who is larger than his Dad.
That's because he can't hunt or fish for himself yet.
He's very fat, but after awhile, he will slim down.
He won't get a white head until he's five or so.
His Mom is larger than his Dad because she has to carry those big eggs."

"Come , Grandma. It's so exciting! Firsty is getting ready to fly.
He is flapping his wings so hard! There he goes!
He landed on another tree! Now what will happen?"

"Let's watch and see. He is now crying.
I think he's a little scared and wants to go back to the nest."

"Can't he go fishing when he's hungry?"

"No, Waylon, he doesn't know how to catch a fish.
He will have to go back to the nest for a few weeks whenever
he is hungry, and his parents will bring him food again."

"Can you hear him  crying? He is hungry right now."

"Come, Grandma. I think I see two eaglets now in the nest, but Firsty is out on a branch!"

"You're right, Waylon. I think we have a third eaglet this year. He just showed up. He is called the runt. See how small he is. He is not at all ready to fly."

"Look, Grandma. Firsty is landing on the feeding branch!"

"Yes, Waylon. Now watch what happens. Firsty is landing on the feeding branch, and now both of his parents are there, too. I think that this is like a bird cafeteria. Look, the Mom is passing part of a fish to Firsty."

"I wonder how Runty is doing, Grandma? "

"He just fledged yesterday.
Fledged means he flew away from the nest."

"Waylon, you are watching a real drama for this poor little eagle. He was trying to return to the nest to be fed, but he landed on a branch way below the nest. Now he is stuck!  I hope that he figures out that he can't fly straight up. There is no elevator in the tree."

"What will Runty do? He is crying so much.
Can we help him?"

"No, Waylon. We'll just have to wait. He should
figure out that he needs to fly away from the tree
and then come back towards the nest at a higher level."

"But he's crying so much, and he is hungry.
The whole family is eating dinner in the nest,
and he is stuck on a branch below the nest."

"Sometimes birds or animals can't figure things out,
but we hope that Runty does."

"Look, Grandma. Runty is back in the nest, and he's not crying."

"Wonderful, Waylon. We're happy that he learned what to do, and that he isn't hungry any more."

"Grandma, why are all
three eaglets crying?
They are on the feeding branch
with Mom, and they are crying."

"Well, Waylon, this is the end of their Mom giving food to them. Now, they have to learn how to hunt and fish by themselves."

"She is showing them that she doesn't have any fish for them. They will cry all day. And tomorrow all of them will be gone."

"Gone? Where will they go?"

"Up the Skagit River where there are plenty of salmon spawning in the river. There are enough salmon for many eagles there."

"But won't they come back? Isn't Samish Island their home?"

Salish Sea

Bellingham Bay

SAMISH ISLAND

Alice Bay

Padilla Bay

"The parents will come back in October. They will return to the nest. They start adding sticks to the nest in the Winter, and then they will have more eaglets that we can see in May. This couple will live a long time, and they will return to Samish Island year after year.

I have been watching them for eleven years, and I have seen twenty-five eaglets in that nest!

Waylon, you can come back in May and start watching again."

"Sounds perfect, Grandma. I'll be here."

"I came home to Samish Island in 2001 after a multi-year world-oriented birding odyssey, and found amazing beauty in my back yard. While doing yoga on our deck, I noticed an eagle starting to build a nest in the fir trees next door. Another neighbor, Kris Goodan, was also watching these eagles from the other side. Year after year, they added to their nest and fledged new eaglets. Kris has done a masterful job of documenting the (hopefully) annual cycle of this nesting pair of Bald Eagles. From her back yard vantage point on Samish Island, the eastern-most San Juan Island in the Salish Sea, Kris takes us on a rhythmic journey through the calendar cycle of nesting. In 2014, Kris' grandson was born and eventually started noticing these eagles as well.
"Come Grandma!" illustrates this ongoing journey in time."

Thais Armstrong, Artist